For Len Hollywood.
with best wishes.
BoB

Total Immersion

Robert Davidson

Cromarty 2004

SCOTTISH CONTEMPORARY POETS SERIES

SCOTTISH CULTURAL PRESS

First published 1998
by Scottish Cultural Press
Unit 14, Leith Walk Business Centre
130 Leith Walk
Edinburgh EH6 5DT
Tel: 0131 555 5950 • Fax: 0131 555 5018
e-mail: scp@sol.co.uk

British Library Cataloguing in Publication Data
A catalogue for this book is available from the British Library

ISBN: 1 898218 95 1

The publisher acknowledges subsidy from the Scottish Arts Council
towards the publication of this book

THE SCOTTISH ARTS COUNCIL

Printed and bound by
Cromwell Press Ltd, Trowbridge, Wiltshire

Scottish Contemporary Poets Series
(for further details of this series please contact the publishers)

James Aitchison, *Brain Scans;* 1 898218 91 9
Tom Bryan, *North East Passage;* 1 898218 57 9
Gerry Cambridge, *The Shell House;* 1 898218 34 X
Ken Cockburn, *Souvenirs and Homelands;* 1 898218 93 5
Jenni Daiches, *Mediterranean;* 1 898218 35 8
Robert Davidson, *Total Immersion;* 1 898218 95 1
Valerie Gillies, *The Ringing Rock;* 1 898218 36 6
Stanley Roger Green, *Waiting for the Mechanic;* 1 898218 94 3
William Hershaw, *The Cowdenbeath Man;* 1 898218 68 4
Brian Johnstone, *The Lizard Silence;* 1 898218 54 4
Anne MacLeod, *Standing by Thistles;* 1 898218 66 8
Angus Martin, *The Song of the Quern;* 1 898218 92 7
Ken Morrice, *Talking of Michelangelo;* 1 898218 56 0
Siùsaidh NicNèill, *All My Braided Colours;* 1 898218 55 2
Walter Perrie, *From Milady's Wood;* 1 898218 67 6
Maureen Sangster, *Out of the Urn;* 1 898218 65 X
Kenneth C Steven, *The Missing Days;* 1 898218 37 4

Contents

Robert Davidson was born in Glasgow but now lives in Dingwall in Ross-shire where he works in the water industry. He lives in a flat overlooking the Cromarty Firth where he mightily enjoys the view. He is Secretary of the Neil Gunn Memorial Trust.

By the same author:

The Bird and the Monkey

For Maggie

Acknowledgements

Many of the poems here collected in book form have already appeared elsewhere and I happily acknowledge the editors of *Broken Fiddle, Chapman, Coracle, Lines Review, NorthWords* and *Understanding* magazines without whom this boat would have sunk long ago.

In addition to the poems in the above periodicals 'In the Night I Rise' appeared as a limited edition print in the Highland Printmakers' exhibition *WordWorks* together with an inspired modern sculpture by the artist Freddie Robins. 'Undecidit' won *The Sand Garden* competition and both 'Where God is Found' and 'Benediction' were first published in *Pushing The Boat Out,* Kathy Galloway (ed.) (Wild Goose Publications, Glasgow 1995) and are reproduced by permission. 'Fifty years after...' was requested by Highland CND and read at a tree planting ceremony in Dingwall. Loren Eiseley's essay 'The Star Thrower' can be found in his famous collection *The Unexpected Universe.*

I also acknowledge my debt to family and friends too numerous to name but especially to friends Ann and Kerr Yule who assisted with the selection of these poems. An especially deep bow to the Writers in Residence scheme of the former Ross and Cromarty District Council. It was Thom Nairn who first asked: 'But what about the muse, Bob?' and Brian McCabe who carried on where Thom left off.

Swallows

Wild hunters of the summer's lower air
cut through the heat, the fecund daytime hush,
and each bird has its particular prey
chosen by sight – then taken on the rush.

With cap tilted downward against the light
I watch and wonder at their quick turnings,
the co-ordinating of eye to flight,
the lethal exactness of their angled wings.

Then, with surprise, note – it seems important,
closing on their prey the wings become still.
Sight is all! They trust the air to hold them
true to their chosen line, in to the kill.

With each cut another insect's taken
by means as graceful as they are precise.
I despair! Can it be faith that's lacking
this troubled wanderer, dry earthbound scribe?

From My Window

Seven nights I've slept here
and every day a different view.

The estuary is the big picture, I guess,
with its migrant graylags, its salmon
and its wandering, hungry seals.
With the tide in there is a pleasing fullness.
With it out, the islands are revealed.

Along the Firth...there's the causeway
with car lights streaming across
and oil rigs behind
and Invergordon and my friend, Dan,
with his arthritis and his mad laugh,
his defiant turn of mind.

Thrawn.

This building cuts out most of the town,
but there's the old court and the ferry
and the cul-de-sac where, just about now,
Moira will be sitting down
to beaver away at one of her novels,
stretching sometimes, looking out
and far away, to the Strathfarrar hills.

Grand coffee this.

Dougald is out early, turning over his field
against the cold weather to come.
Gulls behind the plough,
rich pickings on such good ground.

The sun comes up over Mount Eagle.
See the mist rise? This time of year
the light is like cold iron.

Mother and Daughter

The stones they picked their way across were round,
shifting dangerously beneath their feet
as mother and daughter made their way down
across the tide line of their strange new beach.

'If not for you I'd be alone,' said Mother.
'I never really believed he would go.'
Then daughter's grip tightened like her lover's
as he stiffened within her in love's throes.

'Has she guessed I forced him out?' Mother thought.
'In spite of his promise perhaps he's told.'
Her daughter's face was clear. It held the sort
of innocence that can't be bought or sold.

'You must talk, my dear, when you are with him.
Tell me if he speaks of me with kindness.'
Daughter continued as though deaf and dumb,
leading her mother on in silence

until, at last, they reached the water's edge
and stood together, gazing, hand in hand.
There Daughter put a hard question to her,
'Mum, are you in love with another man?'

A wave touched her foot as she played for time.
When she could wait no more she answered, 'No,
but if there was another, would you mind?'
A quick reply, 'Yes!' The girl's voice was cold.

Then Mother looked down at her daughter's face
and in the haunted silence watched it change.
Her voice was barely warmer when she said,
'Perhaps it would depend upon the man.'

At this, Mother felt such relief within
she could not see that something good had died
for Daughter had, this way, assumed control,
gripping her tight by her fear and desire.

This is how it is on the waveswept beach
where innocence and love died for all three.
No more comfort or trust and no more peace,
the child leads them on by the cold, gray sea.

The Tay – a verse sequence
(for Ann and Kerr Yule)

At the estuary

Between high and low water, a father observes
cormorants, shags and a few other, seldom seen visitors
to this coast.

His oldest girl lifts a shell and he moves in close.
On their knees, heads bowed and hands over backbones,
they intimately discuss.

His youngest girl squints in jealousy, vector of love and fear,
as Mother draws her close and down to a salt pool, observing
ancient beginnings.

Above the tidal wrack their middle girl contemplates
backs curved like boulders, picks her way across
higher, drier ground.

On the Loch Tay hills

Each day of this long summer and into dun coloured autumn an artist labours up these slopes, crouched over a stick. Burdened monstrously by a leaning tower of easel and stand, paints, brushes and telescope, he finds his unitary subject and strives for perfection through detail. From road to summit.

Giving particular attention to background, hard basic textures, he contrasts living forms, lured from their dark hideaways by light, with stone. Purple saxifrage he finds to be more pink. Holly fern innumerably leaved, leaves endlessly serrated. He takes great care with the petals and stamens, anxious to capture their vital, sexual qualities.

At last, on a high shoulder of this elevated, rolling landscape, he makes his studio and attempts the whole picture finding, alas, his sense of perspective is gone. The summation of all this detail is unity to a divine hand only. In momentary bitterness he slashes down and across and again, a cross. Snaps his brush.

Unburdened at last he walks freely over the tops, looking on great houses, fields, reeking chimneys, the marks of his kind on the land. And through it all there is the river, its surface patterns lost to the eye but its larger purpose clearly apparent. Drawing all wetness unto itself it carries the land, in tiny instalments, through Perth and Dundee to the sea.

In Strathfillan

Fair Duncan, of the people of the carpenter,
over from Glen Orchy, shelters from the rain
behind the wall of the graveyard of St Fillan.
Recalling the great songs he has made for this land
and the small songs he has made to keep
a smile on the face of his master he
snuffles up through hairy nostrils and thinks,
Eh! The e teanga airgead gu bheil a h-annam. *

For twenty years he has worked these hills and glens
with his stalker's eye and his poet's accuracy and
it seems to him that though he has its parts,
its berries and flowers, its deer, the fay creatures,
he has not yet grasped the whole of the Misty Corrie.
Now he is to be parted from the land and the thought
would break the heart behind this stone wall but then,
Cha bhi mi a'cuir pogan air an t-airst
               aig an Diuc Araghaidheal! **

* *Ah! I've got a silver tongue in me.*
** *I will not be planting kisses*
               on the arse of the Duke of Argyll.

To the source

The Tay, which had become the Fillan,
turns again to become the Cononish and
moving against the flow we see away
to our left, Scots Pines waiting, waiting.
Notwithstanding the teeming rain that
is whipped around us by the wind
the river narrows and grows thin until
we can cross it with a comfortable stride
at a last turn near the head of the Glen
and up in a high corrie of Beinn Laoigh find
the highest permanent standing water that
is the Tay at its start, its very beginning.
Looking down from the ridge, pool and river
seem like nothing so much as a human seed
somehow swum up to penetrate the mountain,
its slender tail sinuous, roiling –
                    seething with life!

Young Girl Coiling Your Hair

(for Natalie Raulo)

Young girl coiling your hair, finger and thumb,
seated like an angel fallen to earth.
How well you look among the ferns and broom.

Please excuse an old man's admiration
and let me watch you. It's been so long since
I viewed such loveliness. An old man's patience

can be sore tried these intolerant days.
When a man gets to my age, you know, he
sees in a different way the pretty face,

the lovely form of one like you. This hill,
and I've loved it all my life, is complete
only with your presence. For whom do you wait?

Not for one like me, of course! Yet my gift,
I believe, you will someday treasure more
than a younger man's flattery. Resist,

please, any thoughts of a sexual motive
in what I have to say for I am moved,
at my age, well into life's broader view.

You see, I remember you from the past.
Like the broom and the ferns you are repeated,
because of you there can be no 'at last'.

Skin, eyes, face, and the very way you sit,
all of these things are wonderful, it's true.
Seeing you there I know you simply fit.

You hold the future. I can't see past you.

A Fisherman's Song for Attracting Seals

Swim in, swim in, through the spume and the mist.
Fisher folk know seals love sweet music too.
Come, listen to my song. Come feel my kiss.

Old men tell me, knowing seals from the first,
on land you are women with breasts and womb.
Come, listen to my song. Come feel my kiss.

To you I sing of a lonely man's wish
for homestead and children, fireside and book.
Swim in, swim in, through the spume and the mist.

Leave the storms behind, the hunger for fish.
A lifetime of plenty awaits if you'll
come. Listen to my song, come feel my kiss.

The sea is fearful cold, the land is blessed.
You know not what awaits those bold ones who
swim in. Swim in, through the spume and the mist.

Here is an open hand, here a clubbed fist.
My nets are torn and my fishes are few.
Swim in, swim in, through the spume and the mist,
Come, listen to my song. Come feel my kiss.

From the Deep

The memory
of desire.

I was young and my wish
was to live by the sea
in a whitewashed bothy,
its back to the mountains,
its panelled walls
warmed by a peat fire
that left its whisky smell
on the donkey jacket
I wore to the beach in winter,
crunching across shingle,
turning over stones,
examining tidal pools.

The unmade man
remembers love.

Now I recall
other beaches,
walking by moonlight,
foolish thoughts,
waking together,
the sound of the sea,
making love,
and love, I tell you,
love,
making us.

The consummation
of solitude.

At dusk I would raise the wick
of the bothy's lamp
and sit by the upended door
that was my desk,
my left hand
steadying the paper,
my pen laughing and dancing
across the page,
an island of light,
an ocean of darkness,
another light rising,
the moon over the water.

The destination
of experience.

Listening to the wind
and the breaking surf
I might blow
through the palm
of a fingerless glove.
That imagined warmth...

                      ...Rachael
dropping a long held stone
into the same palm,
her child's warmth,
the heart of my hand,
the descent of the stone
into the depths.

The monster Truth
in the Sea of Dreams.

Tonight I look from the window
across this endless sea
that is fed by books and memories.
A dark fluke parts the surface
and...

         a great boiling...
the Creature leaps like Leviathan
rising from the Book of Isaiah,
fixing the bothy with its gaze,
its unforgiving stare,
piercing and pinning me,
relentlessly holding,
constraining me.

A Glass of Pure Water
after a conversation one Friday night
(for Tom McGrath)

Hold a glass of pure water to the light
and what do you see, one thing or two?
It may be the water will elude your sight
and the brittle glass seem the entire truth
its ovoid base completely fill your view.

What then of the clear and perfect fluid
that fills the glass to its very brim
and adopts its shape as its external truth?
Well, there's more to water than its outer form
for when the light hits, so, it seems to blaze alone.

Tom, how very like the mind and the soul
which are so rarely perceived as one.
Each part seemingly has its own separate role
and, functioning apart, apparently dwells alone
so that each to each remains unknown.

Yet the empty glass will more easily break
its strength comes mainly from what's inside
and its very existence is for its content's sake,
contents which, when spilled, cannot abide
in any form at all, nor magnify the light!

Now, before you put that glass of water down,
do you still see it as you did at the start?
Content and container, while two, are as one,
so like the unity of light and matter,
or that of the mind and its questing heart.

Oh, Ease Ma Sperit
(efter Hugh MacDiarmid)

*For ilkane at up-heizes himsel will be hummelt, an ilkane at hummles himsel
will be up-heized.*
                St Luke

Oh, ease ma sperit yet again frae the dool
o inwart luikin an pridefu sel-regaurd,
that aye imputs atween essence an the infinite
ma ain sad-wantin ego, an impenetrible baur.

An lay this ignorant saul doon kensome
o the furthest flung bouns the hairn cuid touch,
where a ma thochts, feelins an flesh are jined
as in ma darlin's bouer, penetratin an engulfed.

The Guru's Crisis

We always looked to you for courage,
following your long stick and cloak
along roads we could not have dreamed of,
to stand agape and open palmed with wonder.

Your discourse was a cleansing thing.
The fine gleanings from your life of reading
like scraps of colour in a church window
together made a clearer, brighter Universe,

with all the fear swept away. Listen man,
it's still you we look to for courage.
Mind we raised the stone with ropes and levers?
Mind we planted forests with our bare hands?

Mind the weans' faces when we opened the soil?
Mind the war we fought against the Maggot Men?
Your reasoning was pointed, your decisions like
the sharp *chink!* of a chisel on Caithness slab.

Your heart then was a torch lifted in a pyramid,
your mind a bright light passing between stars.
Young hands place the sacred quaich on your lips.
Drink deep! It's you we look to now for courage.

Celtic Knot

(meditation on an illuminated manuscript)

What kind of mind conceived you, green serpent,
curling on your bed of opulent gold?
It gave you a wickedly thoughtful eye
and gifted your tail to your mouth to hold.
Are you more than a beast of ill intent
awaiting its moment to strike and fly?

Serpent, you are a symbol of wisdom,
and always thus from the earliest days.
And yet your knot is untied at peril,
only the brave or foolhardy would dare.
Monkish hands formed you but from what model,
something older than Christ? Yes, older still!

Where stands wisdom without intelligence,
or intelligence without hard, straight truth?
This book, this *world*, is perceived in the mind,
rounded off, made acceptable and good.
That same mind works in me now, so intense
it precludes all doubt of on-going life.

Here I pause for I know all things must end
including life itself and not just mine.
All that remains will be what was begun;
dust, gas and energy – nothing divine
but abstract truth for no lie could withstand
the holocaust that leaves Creation dumb.

Truth consumes all and is itself consumed.
Intelligence is its recognition
as acceptance is the only wisdom.
The mind that placed you in this condition,
could it have been as intricate as you?
Why this complex, enigmatic system?

Dare I untie your knot? I don't think so,
living in hope is complicated art.
Monk or poet, the mind averts its sight
from straightforward truth, seeing just the part
embracing life when death completes the whole.
I fear you, serpent, fear your sudden bite.

The Swift

Perthshire! The loveliest of the many places
that we have left our lifetimes' traces.
Aye, marks scratched lightly on sand.
She halted on our walk,
                    touched me with a hand
that was cooler than the evening air.
I could not face her. The depth of her despair
cannot be plumbed by man.

            All around us, and at such speed,
            swifts hunted insects through the trees.
            'They can barely walk,' I told her.
                            'In fact they merely cling.
            The secret of such grace
                            is to live life on the wing.'

She would not be deflected though her voice
was shaking. She spoke as one who had no choice.
'At fifty I should not feel this way,
and me with two big sons!
                    And yet I cannot stay
this grief. All I have, but them, I'd give
to carry life again. I would give birth
but can't. All I know is pain.'

            In hospital the strain showed on her face
            for, in her choice, she felt she had betrayed
            a third, unconceived child.
                            I reminded her once more
            of the perpetual bleeding
                            and the pain she had before.

'Oh, you! Trust you to be rational,' she said,
lightly. But I knew she still heard in her head
the rumble of the trolley on the long, slow ride
from gynae to theatre.
                    Then she lengthened her stride
as though to leave me, till suddenly she missed
a step for, close by a rowan tree, a swift
lay stunned and on its side.

            It is not in her, and never was,
            to pass a lost, but still living, cause.
            She knelt and eased it gently
                        into her quickly emptied bag
            and there it lay, as still
                        as death in the womb-like dark.

She climbed to the top of the nearest rise
where, with both hands, she reached inside
to close them slowly, as one at prayer,
around the frightened swift.
                    She stood tall there
and raised it high then, at her topmost reach,
opened her palms and felt it stretch
as it tried to catch the air.

            It tumbled from her hands, one beat, two, three,
            then, with infinite grace, flew toward the trees.
            And her voice trailed after, 'The choice
                        is always life or death,'
            as her arms came slowly down
                        and her heels returned to earth.

Fossil Light

You cannot live in the present
for awareness lags just behind.
All sensed is experience remembered,
the present is the past dismembered

and selected from so we can live
with ourselves, moderate our guilt,
and consider our sins as from afar
that are as present...
                                   as light from the stars!

The Star Thrower
(Remembering Loren Eiseley)

In the chill hour before dawn torches
hover on the tideline like firefly lights.
I dress in the dark and make my way
across the sands to the starfish kettles
to watch as beautiful, voiceless creatures
are boiled alive, as the shells are cleansed.
      Here to the beaches of Costabel
I have come unknowing of myself,
voided of pity, hope and meaning
by the emetic grip of endless analysis.
Stripped down by years of learning and thought
to no more than an eye fixed within a skull,
I make my footprints on the sands of the littoral,
look back at the dreadful tide and hurry on.

At the foot of a shimmering rainbow,
where rain and spray are joined,
a ragged figure searches,
throws live starfish out to sea.
'The living stars throw well,' he calls.
'If the offshore pull is strong enough
                    they may live.'

The eye in the terrible skull fixes on him
for it perceives only chaos and anti-chaos.
Although form is illusion and
           all sentience reduces to animalcule,
there is a struggle between what is
and what is to be.
               Under the shadow of chaos
form cleaves unto itself stubbornly
for change is, at first, destructive.
Life is metamorphic and homeless,
counter movements in a game of risk
that cannot be influenced by rolling bones
                  or sacrifices.

Progress is an unstoppable wave
with, on its crest,
the interlocked and evolving web of life.
Individuals do not matter!
Starfish and man are one.

Ah, Man! – specialist in cruelty,
                    what of your mind?
Ghostly with transformations, mutations,
and banshee memories of a forest you cannot leave!

Good and evil, lying occult within Him,
have haunted Man since antiquity
and persist in Science in other guises.
I must get back to the beginning,
locate the start of this division.
But standing on the tangle of all that ever was,
looking back through the generations
                    and species,
I find my gaze arrested by the compassionate eye
of my own mother which, in humanity,
I cannot pass.
Here I am. I can see neither back nor forward,
only stare at wreckage.

The Star Thrower straightens,
blesses me with his broken-toothed smile,
and the shore resounds
                    with the crashing of illusions.
Out of desolation emerges the freedom to choose
and in that choice freedom and chaos
resume their conflict.

I pick up a star whose tube feet venture
                    timidly among my fingers
while it cries soundlessly for life.
Nothing gazes on Nothing and is not content
while up ahead the Star Thrower
gropes around beneath his rainbow.

I watch soaked as this creature of desolation
stretches out its hand in pity
and my star spins out over the waves.
'I understand,' I shout.
                    'Call me another thrower.'

Here on the beaches of Costabel I feel
the closing of a circle in my mind at last.
I throw again and, out on the rim of the Universe,
imagine another star seized and flung.
Across the abyss,
                    another galaxy spins more joyfully.
I throw and throw again as,
                    away on the edge of everything,
a ragged, broken-toothed god also throws
and grins his gambler's grin.
'If the offshore pull is strong enough
they may live.'

Sonnet: written after our parting

Thus was separation proved a process
and not an isolated incident.
Or a winnowing of self, more or less
reduction, a solitary intent
doomed to fail.
                   For the nature of the soul
is like that of droplets of moisture
that seek other drops when the air grows cold,
to cling together and be so inured
against the freezing emptiness all around,
drawing ever closer to share their warmth
until that closeness feels like being drowned,
or lost in the mist that has been thus formed.

Until, the end of their integration,
they are sprung apart by surface tension.

Luve, Fund Like Tormentil oan the Heich Hill

Peerie gowden flooers scattered like coin
I come across as wi ma last braith,
climbin an searchin fur somethin else,
silence or peace or…ach, jist escape.

I gang clase an claser still tae touch
jaggit leaves saft oan ma finger,
fower braw petals an thur stamen.
Weel named, *'erecta'*. Prood wee thing.

In times by, used fur the easement o pain,
or sae I'm tellt. Noo, I draw furth the root
tae find it's rid, rid as hert's bluid
an…*whit's this?*…swersh in the mooth!

Undecidit

Whit's she weighin up?
        Her luve an her worth.
The mune hings heich
        ower the Beauly Firth.

An whit's that soun,
        is someone oan the wey?
Burdies, turnin in thur sleep
        at the hush o day.

Which wey tae gang when
        thur's nocht but fear abroad?
The road oan which she's gangin's
        a singul treck road.

Gie in, mak luve? But she's
        a dacent sense o sin!
Ah, the stirrin an the fechtin
        o thae things deep within.

Her heid's birlin, so's her hert.
        She can barely staun!
Come here, ma lassie, close tae me.
        I want tae haud yer haun.

In the Night I Rise

In the night I rise in my dreaming mind
to look on myself asleep. Below lies
an awful sight for my shattered ribcage
has been prised apart as by one enraged.

And it is a horror to me, this scene,
until I set my gaze by force of will,
for then I see that ribs are much like trees
and that lungs fill like bushes with the wind.

It is like a forest glade in the night,
all silent and still, where no beating wing
disturbs the air nor timid creature starts.
Nothing but me moves so much as an eye
until I pick out that elegant thing,
a hind – and she's drinking deep from my heart.

Four Marriage Haiku

A sudden death

The phone slides down my
chest, carries my hand with it.
Her hand clasps my arm.

On the rocks

In a lounge and not
trying to please. She says: *Don't
hold your glass that way!*

The way we were?

He commands, she defers.
He decides, she enacts.
Enacting, she commands.

In the dark

I awake afraid
and for no reason she turns.
Her arm snakes round me.

Sanctus

My luve is like the Holy Ghost,
I kenna when she comes or goes.

I only ken when we are twined,
the cannle's licht within my mind.

I only feel when we're apairt,
the cannle's warmth within my hert.

My luve is like the Holy Ghost,
she passes through me and I'm lost.

What is the Colour of Movement?

…read a note taped to his studio wall
near a long canvas of contrived chaos
that was not representative at all.
I asked cautiously what this canvas was.

Brushes in jars, and paint, lay all around
but he saw them not. The painting's design
took intense concentration – shapes, some round,
some edged, and colours balanced by his mind.

'You may think me large, but pictures are tricks
called forth to astonish the innocent.
You say a child could paint this way? *Agreed!*
To lay down all acquired culture, like this,
and grow anew is my aim.' I laughed then,
the colour of movement is bright indeed.

for Dean Melville

Scottish Folk Song and the World of Work

On rail lines your mind will run. We
will use education to narrow your guage
and drive you where you would not go.

Oh, would I were where Helen lies,
or could grow wings an tak tae the skies.

You will never ease your face into the light
but always be looking down at your hands.
Your eyesight will weaken and your back will hurt.

Westering home and a song in the air,
Islay's distilleries, I'll tak ma ease there.

Money will always be short for you and yours.
Every time you feel you are getting on top
something will haul you back. We will ensure this.

Is there for honest poverty, that hings his heid an a that?
Oh aye! an he's felt for lang his life might never start.

You will grow to hate your job so intensely
rising in the morning will be an act of will,
and yet you will fear its loss as death itself.

Where are the joys I met in the morning?
Turned in the evening tae desperate longing.

You will take your job to be your survival
and give it so much of yourself your children
will be like strangers and come to despise you.

Cauld blaws the evenin blast, when bitter bites the frost
yet I believe, wi a ma hert, that luve is never lost.

If you are lucky you will wait out your last years
in quiet, anxious submission, but without want.
Our triumph will be your belief that this is right.

Fareweel ye dungeons dark and strang, the wretch's destiny.
I'll tak sic time as I can hae, an never bow the knee.

High on the Steppe

Night, and the dacha is ablaze with light,
an island in an ocean of snow. Has
anywhere ever been so isolated?

The doctor is at his desk, pen in hand.
A growing pile of papers on the floor
is the fruit of his labour. Poetry!

He is blinking down, frowning, writing fast,
while distant hoofbeats echo in his head.
Irregular cavalry on the way,

but whether from the past or the future
he cannot tell. Now the song of the wolf
hangs eerie in the night. He lifts his face

but has no time to become anxious
as she enters with a load of firewood
and drops it carelessly in a corner.

Not looking at him she sweeps back her hood
and lights another candle. He scribbles,
'...that reflects from the snow on her lashes',

then looks at his pen as I look at mine.
You know, I have enough – don't envy much
but, Pasternak – your gift for dreaming dreams!

Myth

(beginning with two lines by Thom Gunn)

I prowl the labyrinthine corridors
   and have a sense of being underground
but still it is my life that I endorse,
   those vital fragments that sound and resound
like the darkbound echo of an old song
   heard only when it is least expected.
Is there some law that says you must wait long
   for those moments that lift you from the dead?
Moments like flames.
                Moments like singing wires
   heard by a blind man as he grasps the air
with helpless hands, gazing with inward eyes.
   On this stumbling journey such times are rare:
loved ones grow older, lose their strength and die,
   sleepless nights of worrying never end,
mind numbing toil is endured for money,
   the labyrinth is all darkness ahead.
Yet still it is my life that I endorse.

   As I make my way with no bright thread
to guide me a snatch of song goes before
   and I follow on with hesitant tread
to the centre, the lair of the godbeast.
   His is a still presence, dark as midnight,
glaring down on me with a livid heat,
   when sounds a bellcall from the far outside
that turns and carries in heedless ascent.
   The nightingale's song goes straight to the soul.

Now the godbeast raises his heavy head,
   his long horns and thick neck, his broad, wet nose,
and from somewhere deep in his sacred part
   a voice like the risen Christ emerges
in answer until the labyrinth's heart
   resounds with huge symphonic arias,
lyric refrains in unvarying time,
   soaring cadenzas, high triumphant chords,
moments like flames, widening pools of light;
   and still it is my life that I endorse.

One Tongue

Eskill Romme, playing the Castle with Suleskaer,
fidgeting awkwardly before a dozen or so listeners,
bides his time while
        Scandinavian dance music goes
jiggly-jig, jiggly-jig, jiggly-jig
then picks up a tiny straight sax and blows through
that jiggly-jig, jiggly-jig, jiggly-jig
a soprano sound of such poignancy that,
amongst all that Folk,
              folk lean forward. Listen,
Fred Morrison, playing the Northern Meeting,
at the corner of the stage is playing his *big tune*
        Beloved Scotland
          I leave thee
            broken hearted
and holding that opening cadence so long
it is almost to the detriment of the music. Yet
it is that sound, that extended 'eee',
          that holds us still. Listening
as to Charlie Parker, rising in a spotlight,
high above the smoking ashtray of his life,
leaning far back, rubber spined, with
that big tenor sax curling
        from groin to mouth
         and calling,
           calling out his cry of pain.
Before the tune, beyond all possible technique,
        the union of sound and soul
          breaks the heart and heals it.
Unsigned by time. Scoring through eternity.

Self-Portrait With Picasso Cat *
(Watercolour by John Bellany)

He knows us both so well,
catching my principal characteristics,
my shark's teeth, my smile,
with a few deft, simply executed strokes
before attending to his outer self.

He's shown his eyes as huge and blank.
All feeling and expression rest with me,
this evil humour.
Mine's being the vivisectionist's way
he feeds me the sitter and then stands back.

It's risky, you know, though he's clever indeed.
He knows both eyes and teeth are *di rigeur*
for his art,
but I'll rend his soul like that of a bird
if he gives me no other souls to eat.

* viewed in Aberdeen Art Gallery

Almost a Year After...

(The woman asked for the child back almost a year after handing him over.
– *The Scotsman,* Feb. 1994.)

Pick a side, Your Honour,
but let's have no pretence
of a qualitative assessment
on different loves. No sense

pretending you know what's best
for this one year old bairn.
You have nothing good to offer,
you are a dispenser of pain.

I think it's you I pity most,
as the Law's elevated fool.
Go, search your books for precedent,
locate some kind of rule –

and then swing your axe.

The Bridge
(based on the willow pattern)

daughter

by the water side
how we love to walk this path
        i miss my father

                son

            the cormorant's neck
            stretching in the winter light
                a despairing arm

    mother

their feet on the bridge
hammer beating in my mind
        the foundations shift

           cormorant

          children come with sticks
          bare legs dividing the reeds
             dive to the bottom

     trout

head lies between stones
minnows swimming through its hair
        eyeball in my mouth

          father

          catch the fish children
         sun dry and eat well this night
            with you forever

Induction to Auschwitz

On both sides of the tracks,
as far as the eye could see,
were red and white lights
and two groups of bony puppets
in berets and striped pyjamas.
As they closed and wheeled around us
we understood that this was mad
and that madness was our fate.

In the hour of decision we sensed
what is unknown to the living
and we said farewell to life
by saying farewell to one another.

Strong men with razors fell on us
and, in a moment,
                    we were stripped and sheared.
I had never seen old men naked –
            such dignity in grief and fear.

In an instant our women disappeared
and the historical necessity
of killing the children
became self-evident.
When we men discovered we were alone
our continued survival was reduced
to pointless existence.

The modern hell is to wait
                    in an empty room
when you have been removed
            from the future.

from the memories of Primo Levi

38

Sonnet: written for the early retired

You are wanderers, you early retired.
What happened to your often rehearsed plans,
the people you'd see, the work with your hands?
The streets are hollow and cannot be filled
by your brisk movement, your circular walk.
Is it the ghost of your old life you seek,
while the rhythm of your relentless feet
sweeps away your time like the office clock?

That clock still sits heavy on your shoulders.
It folds and twists you as you make your way
through your endless round. Its white face looks down.
Can you not hear its ironic laughter
as you walk and walk? When you halt and sway,
stumble and fall, its busy hands sweep on.

Restless

Restless, he stares at the computer screen,
moves its cursor and clicks its little mouse,
shifts his eyes to notice the tiny seams
on the back of the hand he stretches out.

That hand once placed a dirk between his teeth
and trailed down a lover's china white back,
drew a rapier for *La Republique,*
piloted a Spit' through enemy flak.

As a boy he had no troubles to seek.
Wrongs to be righted were all around him.
Now he laughs at the memory. How rich,
to believe that he might have changed a thing.

So he turns again to the glowing screen.
Knowing what's best he gives it all his mind,
living for his lunch and the short drive home,
the kiss at the door, the first glass of wine…

This is the way that young men are made old,
with boredom and bottomless cups of tea
and the desperate hollow sound of bones
rattling fleshless and dry by dead, salt seas.

Sonnet: written on my brother's return from Estonia

Ian brought me a bottle of vodka
with a cheap looking label and cap,
a gift from his trip to Estonia.
I stared at it hard.
                    Well, it looked like crap!

But later, when I shared it with my friends
the Baltic bevvy went down like nectar!
So unlike Scotland's favoured grainy blends,
gulped down when they're drowned in a sweetener.
How like him!
                    To hand me such a symbol
for a poorer land that is, at last, free –
the pure spirit and its shabby label.

Later my friends discussed and agreed
that it must surely be the sweetener
worsening the pain of the hangover.

Fifty years after the dropping of the bomb on Hiroshima

Nothing is as it was before,
poison dust sits on every mind.
What happened once will happen again,
the end of all things is visible and known.

Watch that girl as she looks about,
she remembers without ever being told,
the *smack* of the impact, the typhoon wind,
the tower of dust turning inside out.

The flash burned deeply into us all
and nothing is done but against a despair
as abiding, damning and obscene as
incinerated children scorched onto walls.

Against that despair, how to make ourselves free?
Hope, being human, survives beyond reason.
The way to live is 'now' and 'soon'.
Time to light a candle. Time to plant a tree.

To My Father

Your life hung like a dislocated
arm.
You'd lost your grip for good.

Now I cover one palm with the other,
one palm with the other,
counting overlaps.

fatherless   childless
        childless   fatherless

Gestures Observed in a Crematorium

Anonymous ministers address temporary congregations
across the unchurched dead.
Sombre spokesmen deliver agnostic eulogies.

    I am limited in my despair,
    there is a danger I may laugh.
    The dead have no need of words,
    theirs is a position of unassailable fact.

Some gestures are important; the dry handshake,
the gripped arm.
What cannot be released remains.

    Endless turnings away
    put nothing behind us.
    We are constantly turning
    towards.

The Sadness is Everywhere

Bombs drift down like snow
and the sadness is everywhere.
    In the eyes of the bereaved
and the swollen stomachs
    of the children of strangers.

News from the wars is mostly good
    but no one comes home.

Mobs of lonely people
            roam the streets,
screaming in unison
but united only by fear.

The sadness is everywhere.

Bombs drift down like snow
and the camps are filling.

All My Hooded Dead

Wakened by the sound of their slow stepping
I watched the dark figures pass my bed,
an endless line, a crowd that kept growing,
my father's people, all my hooded dead.

The room was altered into a vast hall,
an echoless everywhere-at-once
unlit by window, without roof, floor or wall,
that yet was filled by their swaying presence.

They turned towards me, shaking back their hoods
the better to look on me, my dead ones.
And well I knew their faces, their dark looks
that judged me, the last disappointing son.

My father's mother appeared beside me,
a small stout woman in long black dress.
Should I fear her now, this powerful Eve,
who drew my head once more against her breast?

She was the oldest I could remember,
and touchstone of the man I might have been,
that held me close, looking down with pity
and sad love, after all these years alone.

Then she carried me through the parting crowd
past its distant edge, for each one has his place,
his one true place, and there she set me down
to sing the lonely songs of the childless.

Total Immersion

On the wall of my room is the picture of a baptism.
A grown man wholly contained in the arms of another
and both of them in the water.
Both of them in the water with the one in control
and the other trying not to struggle.
It must be very difficult
                      not to struggle.

And then it's down you go.
Down you go!
Total immersion and held down
                          by those powerful arms.
Held down by your own decision
                        not to struggle.
Held down by a powerful desire
                      to be something more,
by a desire to be included in something greater,
by a desire to be infinitely intimate,
by a desire,
by a deep need   to be changed
          by desire.

Eventually you relent and struggle free
or are lost,

lost for good.

The Discovery

As my belief in God diminished
so the pleasure found in prayer increased,

until the idea slowly took hold
that I was alone, myself, quite apart.

Yet as I withdrew the more inwardly,
why, the less I felt myself insecure

until, at the edge of uncertainty,
a hand reached out and fell upon my neck.

Then my soul, deaf singer, still runner, leaped,
and a bright and triumphant laugh rang out.

Clement

It was you who told me of that good man
who was captured and bound to an anchor,
then heaved gunwale-high by a sweating gang
who tipped him over, into the harbour.
And remember, the other thing you told;
the salt sea opened and swallowed him whole.

Ever since then our Christian churches
built harbour-side have taken the saint's name,
Clement, become the spiritual embassies
of sailors in strange lands everywhere.
You know that was why I used to attend;
my life and myself had become estranged.

It seems odd, today I remembered this
when I saw you in your turned-round collar,
black suit and watch-chain, walking in silence
down the High Street. You had a captain's air.
And I recalled your advice, you stated;
Do your best, the rest must be accepted.

You'll never know how hard I tried for both
or how the weight of the anchor shifted
with each heave and step, each pitch of the boat,
or how my heart stopped when I was lifted,
or what it was to plummet like lost love;
and watch the cut rope trailing high above.

Choral Song

Here the turbulent confluence of minds,
the constant adhesion of the soul.
Here the juncture where love defeats time
and steps through the barriers alone.

Choristers are temporary and shed,
discarded chrysalides of butterflies.
Nothing remains below but used up flesh.
Nothing that lives! Here ends 'you and I'.

A higher purpose? We cannot see it,
yet cannot ignore the certainty.
No reason can be intuited
but how we long, *long,* to join and fly.

The Road Tae Bethlehem

'Whit wey's the road tae Bethlehem?'
    a bairn asked me wan morn.
'It's there ma mither waits fur me,
    an am aikin tae be born.'

'The road tae Bethlehem, ma lad,
    is no the road fur ye.
I ken whaur there's a hill o skulls,
    it's there ye'll rest yer heid.'

Frae aff his back I tore his goun
    an watched his sma face fa.
An then I took ma maister's lash
    an whipped his body raw.

Twa nails I fund tae pin his wrists
    fast tae a roadside tree
an frae ma pouch a haund's width spike
    tae batter through his heels.

I stood aneath him till he deed,
    an end baith lang an sair,
but then I heard an aafu soun.
    His voice within ma hairn!

'Oh, I'll live oan within yer hert
    an ye'll live oan tae tell,
an frae the bouns o naethingness
    I will loe ye still.'

Every Step of the Way

(Stabat Mater)

The first steps you took led away from me
and I encouraged them, every one.
A mother's pride contains a mother's fears,
she holds to her place and sends forth her sons.

You went early where I could not follow,
the Books, the Law, the lineage of men,
then, in debate, I heard you'd shut the book,
hard, in the High Priest's face. You'd drawn your line.

The desert called, the leader's lonely way,
and thousands followed. To hear my son speak!
A mother's place does not allow a say,
I bit my tongue when you outstretched your reach.

Your life's desire, the way of the human,
was as nothing to what is and is,
nothing to the hard, metallic token –
and what is *holds*, and must be ruthless.

Drops of blood like flames run across your brow.
A mother's love contains a mother's grief
behind dry eyes. I will not leave you now,
nor yet will I unman you with my tears.

The Sound of Iona

(for Kathy Galloway)

On the road from Kintra I dream of another Church
precariously balanced between what is
and what we make of it,
founded on how we understand
what little of the past we remember.
A Church that does not know where it is going
but is certain that its present condition
is no condition to stay in.

An evolutionary Church is what we require,
that sets every ritual it uses
against its relevance in the world today
and is prepared to discard it all
without consideration of its possible relevance
in any other world.
A Church that is well able to adapt its posture
protectively around the murmuring body of the poor,
effectively countering
the shifting aggressions of the rich
and that is, at last, done with excuses.
A Church that fundamentally understands that
if frailty is not held sacred, power never can be.

This is the crying need of our people!
A Church that is fully aware
that love is a force
and that peace is its way, not its end,
…but that has discovered new ends
already defined within Nature,
toward which it is prepared to work steadily.
        Give them a Church without respect,
that is anxious to demolish utterly
any part of its own corpus
which stands against these achievements
or obstructs the rapid integration
of all unnecessary and hindering divisions.

This Church I seek is elemental, basic
persistent, sufficient and, therefore, familiar.
Growing older now, in my recall
it seems to me that beginnings are best.
We meet best when we meet as strangers
and that is how this Church and this Man
must enter one another.

At night the road from Kintra is a quiet place.
I pause and listen to the silence,
understanding at last that silence can never be complete.
Always there is the push and pull of the sea,
                              Iona's deepest bell.

Where God is Found

A ball rises until the force driving it up
exactly equals that of gravity and,
for a moment, hangs absolutely still.
A perfect sphere. In that moment,
that's where God is found.

An infant takes a few faltering steps,
then looks up with a big two toothed smile.
In that moment of looking up,
God's there.
And when the first of those teeth
splits the gum. In that parting,
just there.

When lover's eyes meet, God's there.
And when they unlock for good,
just before the first tear wells up
and spills over the lower lid, yes,
there too.

You settle down with a book and
find yourself captured. That moment,
just before you realise,
is where God is found.
Round about page twenty.

Then, while you're reading, you feel
someone looking at you from behind and
you raise your eyes, all uncertain,
and look round.
Not when you turned your head,
or even when you had that feeling,
but when your concentration broke.
There!

A million million spermatozoa
cluster round an ovum so it looks
like it's coated in suede.

Suddenly one breaks through and
in that instant
the others fall away.
God!

Later when a two cell egg
is tumbling down its tube
there comes the moment when
it adheres to the fallopian wall
and *implants*.
That's where God is.
And when it doesn't,
but tumbles on down and away?
There too!

In self-pity because
grief is mostly self-pity
and God knows all about grief.

Ever know something
but not know how?
How do you think?

In the cusp of a fingernail
and its growth at the quick.
In the turning of the furrow,
and the creaming of the bow-wave.
In the lift of the wing
and the angle of ascent.
God is decisive but elusive,
to be found in time
but leaving traces in space.
And where time and space are one,
there He sings his song of light.

Right here at the tip of my pen
a tiny metal ball
spreads dye across the paper.
Just at the point of contact God,
his robe bunched up in his hands,
is running like hell across the page.

Inside the Womb
(last thoughts of a spermatozoon)

…and now the marriage of ghostly spirals
selects one form from all that might have been,
substance from the surrounding mucus calls
and punches out its features from within.

All at once there is a fluid body,
perfect ears, empty sockets for the eyes,
the beginnings of all things sensory,
the formation of umbilical ties.

My memory is long but fading now
as time grows short – but my task is over.
No need, or inclination, to be sad
as I feel, at last, what I have longed for,
movement, rapid flutters at the centre
as…*miracle!* Another child takes heart.

The New Bairn
(for Fern Urquhart)

May you grow up wild and free
as your name
and as Scotland yet might be.

Drink this freedom deep and then
may your love
have you both give birth again.

Benediction

May all your hopes be sustained
between the wings of seagulls,
and may your fears, before they start,
be taloned fast by eagles.

May curling salmon leap the falls
in the river of your strife,
and pine trees crack with age
in the forests of your life.

May speckled fawns raise their heads
beneath your vaulted blue,
and may the God of frost and stars
be ever more with you.